DATE DUE

7/18

			PRINTED IN U.S.A.

WITHDRAWN

PAPER-MACHE MASKS

Jane Yates

WINDMILL
BOOKS

Published in 2017 by **Windmill Books**, an Imprint of Rosen Publishing
29 East 21st Street, New York, NY 10010

Copyright © 2017 Windmill Books

Developed and produced for Rosen by BlueAppleWorks Inc.

Creative Director: Melissa McClellan
Managing Editor for BlueAppleWorks: Melissa McClellan
Designer: T.J. Choleva
Photo Research: Jane Reid
Editor: Kelly Spence
Craft Artisans: Janet Kompare-Fritz (p. 10, 14, 16, 22, 26 28); Jane Yates (p. 9, 12, 18, 20, 24)

Photo Credits: cover left bergia/Shutterstock; cover right Nanette Grebe/Shutterstock; title page,
Austen Photography; TOC Tatiana Belova/Shutterstock; page tops photka/Shutterstock; p. 4
top left kontur-vid/Shutterstock; p. 4 top right antpkr/Thinkstock; p. 4 middle Freedom_Studio/
Shutterstock; p. 4 bottom left Zerbor/Shutterstock; p. 4 bottom middle Kozini/Shutterstock; p. 4
bottom right Aprilphoto/Shutterstock; p. 5 top Fer Gregory/Shutterstock; p. 5 left to right and top to
bottom: Crackerclips/Dreamstime.com; Danny Smythe/Shutterstock; Austen Photography; rangizzz/
Shutterstock; koosen/Shutterstock; Samantha Roberts/Shutterstock; Texturis/Shutterstock; 6 – 29
Austen Photography

Cataloging-in-Publication Data

Names: Yates, Jane.
Title: Paper-mache masks / Jane Yates.
Description: New York : Windmill Books, 2017. | Series: Cool crafts for kids | Includes index.
Identifiers: ISBN 9781499482348 (pbk.) | ISBN 9781499482355 (library bound) |
 ISBN 9781508192824 (6 pack)
Subjects: LCSH: Papier-mâché--Juvenile literature. | Handicraft--Juvenile literature.
Classification: LCC TT871.Y38 2017 | DDC 745.54'2--dc23

Manufactured in the United States of America
CPSIA Compliance Information: Batch #BW17PK:
For Further Information contact Rosen Publishing, New York, New York at 1-800-237-9932

CONTENTS

GETTING STARTED

Paper-mache, also known as papier-mâché, is an art form that uses paper mixed with glue. This material can be placed on a **mold** or formed by hand to make different shapes. When it hardens, it forms a lightweight, hard surface. This fun art form gets its name from the French words for "chewed paper."

You don't need a lot of materials for paper-mache projects. You can find whatever you need at a craft store or dollar store, or even around the house. You can buy plastic face molds, or make a **base** using balloons, paper plates, or egg cartons. Organize your supplies in boxes or plastic bins. Pull them out when you want to make paper-mache masks!

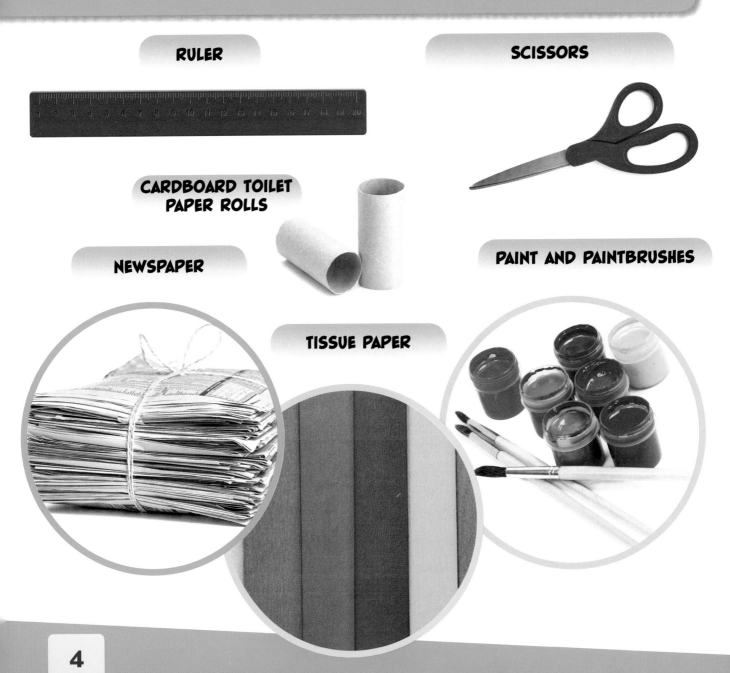

RULER

SCISSORS

CARDBOARD TOILET PAPER ROLLS

NEWSPAPER

PAINT AND PAINTBRUSHES

TISSUE PAPER

WHITE GLUE

Did You Know?

Paper-mache was invented in China. It was used to make **helmets** and dishes. Over time, it was used to make all sorts of things, like dolls, masks, and furniture. Today, it is mostly used for crafts, and to make colorful **piñatas** that are filled with candy!

PAPER PLATES

PLASTIC MOLDS

PAPER TOWELS

FEATHERS

PENCIL

MASKING TAPE

YARN NEEDLE

BALLOONS

A note about measurements

Measurements are given in US format with metric in parentheses. The metric conversion is rounded to make it easier to measure.

TECHNIQUES

Have fun while making your paper-mache masks! Be creative.
Your masks do not have to look just like the ones in this book.
The book shows how to use different kinds of bases. You can
substitute a plastic mask mold for a balloon base if needed.
If you do not have a half-face mold, make one out of cardboard
using the pattern on page 31.

Use the following techniques to create your paper-mache masks.

PAPER-MACHE GLUE - MADE WITH FLOUR

- Add 1 cup (236 grams) of flour and 3 tablespoons (45 g)
of salt to a bowl. Slowly pour in 1 cup (250 milliliters)
of water, mixing with a spoon. Continue to add water
until you have a smooth, thin paste.

PAPER-MACHE GLUE - MADE WITH GLUE

- Add 1 cup (250 milliliters) of white glue and 1 cup (250 milliliters) of water
to a container with a lid. (An empty yogurt container works well.) Mix the
glue and water together with a spoon. If you have leftover glue, you can put
the lid on and use it later.

PAPER-MACHE TECHNIQUE

- Prepare your base. You can make masks out of paper
plates, egg cartons, balloons, or use store-bought molds.

- Tear several strips of newspaper,
tissue paper, or paper towel.

- Mix together your paper-mache glue.

- Use a paintbrush to coat both sides of a strip. Or dip
the strip into the glue, then use your fingers to squeeze
off the extra paste.

- Place the strips one at a time on the mold. Smooth the
strips with your fingers to remove any air bubbles and
extra glue. Crisscross the direction of the strips to
create an even surface. Completely cover the mold.

- Set the mask aside to dry. This usually takes a full day.

Tip

When working with a
balloon, cut a hole in
the middle of a paper
plate. Then, pull the
end of the balloon
through. Use tape to
hold it in place. The
balloon will stay upright
while you work.

HALF-BALLOON MASK

- When the paper-mache dries, use scissors or a needle to pop the balloon. Draw a line down the center of the balloon lengthwise. Cut along the line to make two halves. Each can be used to make a mask.

PAPER-MACHE SHAPES

- To make paper-mache shapes, press together several strips to make a wad. Squeeze out the extra glue, then form the wad into the desired shape. Add it to the base, cover it with more strips, and let it dry completely.

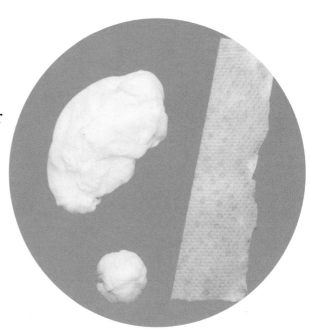

Tip

Paper-mache is messy! Cover your work station with newspaper or a garbage bag.

BE PREPARED

- Read through the instructions and make sure you have all the materials you need.
- Clean up when you are finished making your masks. Put away your supplies for next time.

BE SAFE

- Ask for help when you need it.
- Ask for permission to borrow tools.
- Be careful when using scissors and needles.

ATTACHING YOUR MASK

To attach your mask using elastic cord, measure a cord that will fit comfortably around your head. Add a little extra for securing the ends to the mask. Use the pattern on page 31 if you decide to create you own mask base.

TIED ELASTIC CORD

- Poke a hole on either side of the mask. (A yarn needle works well for this.) Thread one end of the elastic cord through one hole, then make a knot. Repeat for the other side.

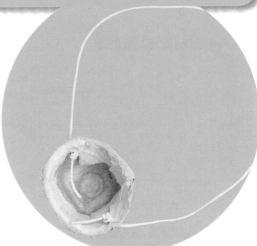

STAPLED ELASTIC CORD

- Ask an adult to help you staple the elastic to each side of the mask.

TAPED ELASTIC CORD

- Cut two small pieces of strong tape. Tape each end of the elastic to the inside edges of the mask.

WOODEN HANDLE

- Make a handle to hold the mask in front of your face. Paint a wooden stick or pencil, then tape it to the side of the mask.

PIG NOSE

You'll Need:

✔ Egg carton
✔ Scissors
✔ Paper towel strips
✔ Paper-mache glue
✔ Paint and paintbrush

1 Carefully cut a single cup out of an egg carton. Trim around the edges to make it an even circle.

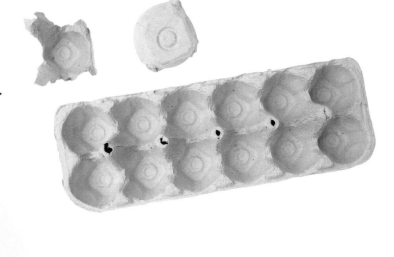

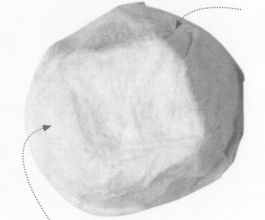

2 Cover the cup with strips of paper towel dipped in the glue mixture. Let it dry.

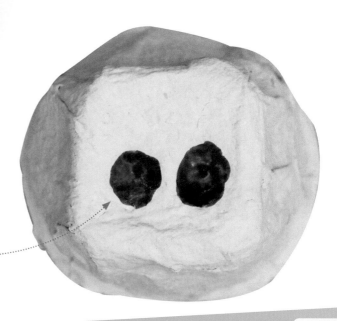

3 Paint the nose. Add two dots for nostrils.

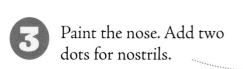

SUPERHERO MASK

You'll Need:

✔ Cardboard
✔ Newspaper strips
✔ Scissors
✔ Tape
✔ Paper-mache glue
✔ Paint and paintbrush
✔ Glitter glue

1 Trace the mask, eyehole, and flame patterns on page 30 onto a piece of paper. Cut out the patterns, then tape them to a piece of cardboard. Follow the pattern to cut out the mask, then cut out the two eyeholes. Set aside the flame pattern.

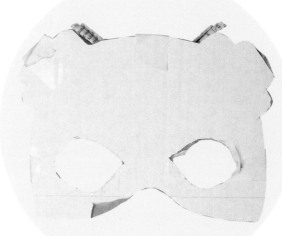

2 Roll up pieces of newspaper to make three-dimensional shapes on the mask. Use tape to attach them. Tape long, twisted rolls around each eyehole.

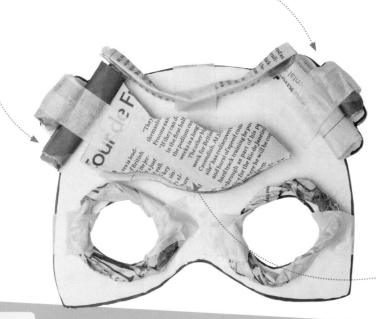

3 Place the flame pattern on a stack of newspaper. Cut around the pattern. Once you have about 10 flames stacked together, tape the stack onto the mask above the eyeholes.

4 Cover the mask with paper-mache. Wrap strips around the sides to cover the edges. Let it dry.

5 Paint the mask.

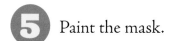

6 Use glitter glue to outline each eye.

Tip

Patience is needed for paper-mache masks. It is important to let each piece dry before moving to the next step.

MASQUERADE MASK

You'll Need:
- ✔ Half-face mask base
- ✔ Newspaper strips
- ✔ Paper-mache glue
- ✔ Paint and paintbrush
- ✔ Fake jewels
- ✔ Glitter glue

1 Start with a half-face mask base.

2 Cover the entire mask with a layer of paper-mache. Set it aside to dry.

3 Paint the mask. Add swirls for decoration. Let it dry.

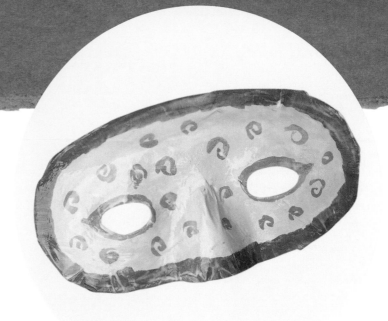

4 Use a paintbrush to cover the entire mask with glue.

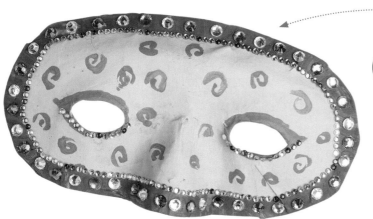

5 While the glue is wet, stick jewels along the edge of the mask. Use smaller jewels to add another row on the inside. Add a line of small jewels under each eye. Let the glue dry.

6 Use another paintbrush to brush glitter glue all over the mask. Add two to three layers. Let the glue dry between each layer.

Tip

Even if you are using fake jewels with a sticky back, use extra glue to help them stick better.

OWL MASK

You'll Need:

- ✔ Half-face mask base
- ✔ Newspaper strips
- ✔ Paper-mache glue
- ✔ Scissors
- ✔ Tape
- ✔ Paint and paintbrush
- ✔ Feathers

1 Trace the ear tufts, cheeks, and beak patterns on page 31 onto a piece of cardboard. Cut out the patterns.

2 Cover the pattern pieces and a half-face mask with paper-mache. Leave to dry.

3 Tape the nose and cheeks onto the mask. Glue the tufts to the top of the mask, just above the eyes.

4 Cover the mask and beak with a second layer of paper-mache. Leave to dry.

5 Paint the mask.

6 Starting at the ends of the tufts, glue three layers of feathers. Each layer should overlap as shown. Add extra feathers under the beak.

LION MASK

You'll Need:

- ✔ Paper plate
- ✔ Cardboard toilet paper roll
- ✔ Scissors
- ✔ Tissue paper
- ✔ Paper-mache glue
- ✔ Paint and paintbrush

1 Draw two eyes on a large paper plate. Use scissors to cut them out.

Cut out ears and teeth

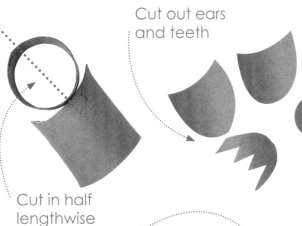

Cut in half lengthwise

2 Cut the toilet paper roll in half lengthwise. Set one half aside. Cut the other piece in half. Cut a semicircle out of each end as shown. Trim one end to make a thin circle for the nose. Use the other half to make ears and teeth.

Cut a semicircle

3 Set the nose below the eyes. Tape the half-tube pieces on an angle below the nose as shown. Scrunch up tissue paper to build up the nose and fill the cheeks. Tape the nose and cheeks onto the mask. For eyebrows, twist a long piece of tissue paper and glue it on above the eyes.

4 Cut several strips of brown tissue paper. Coat each strip with glue, then cover the mask. Use pink tissue paper for the nose.

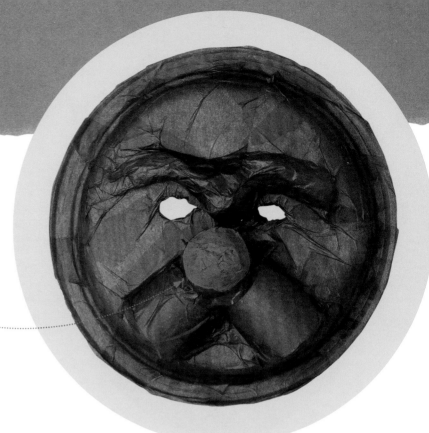

5 Cover the ears in brown and yellow tissue paper. Cover the eyebrows and nose with yellow tissue paper. Use paint to add dots to the mouth and white marks under the eyeholes. Paint the nose red. Glue the ears and teeth on.

6 Cut several 2-inch (5 cm) strips of yellow tissue paper. Glue the strips around the edge of the mask to create the lion's mane. Scrunch up orange tissue paper around the lion's face. Glue the ears and teeth onto the mask.

Tip

Tissue paper rips easily. Brush the glue on rather than dipping it in the glue.

CAMO MASK

You'll Need:

- ✔ Full-face mask base
- ✔ Newspaper strips
- ✔ Paper-mache glue
- ✔ Scissors
- ✔ Paint
- ✔ Moss and leaves (real or fake)

1 Start with a full-face plastic mask.

2 Cover the mask with a layer of paper-mache.

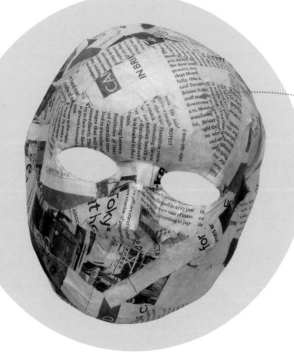

Paint stripes

3 Poke small holes for breathing in the mouth. Paint light green stripes across the mask. Let it dry.

Poke holes

4 Add more stripes using different shades of green and brown paint. Let it dry.

5 Cover the entire mask with glue. Press leaves and moss onto the mask. Make sure you do not completely cover the eyes or mouth. Let it dry.

Tip

Once the mask dries, gently shake it to remove any moss or leaves that did not stick.

MONSTER MASK

You'll Need:

✔ Half-balloon mask base
✔ Scissors
✔ Construction paper
✔ Newspaper strips
✔ Paper-mache glue
✔ Tape
✔ Paint and paintbrush

1 Start with a half-balloon base (see pages 6-7). Draw two eyes and a mouth.

2 Use scissors to carefully cut out the eyes and mouth.

3 To make spikes, roll pieces of construction paper into tubes. Use tape to hold them together. Cut four small slits in one end.

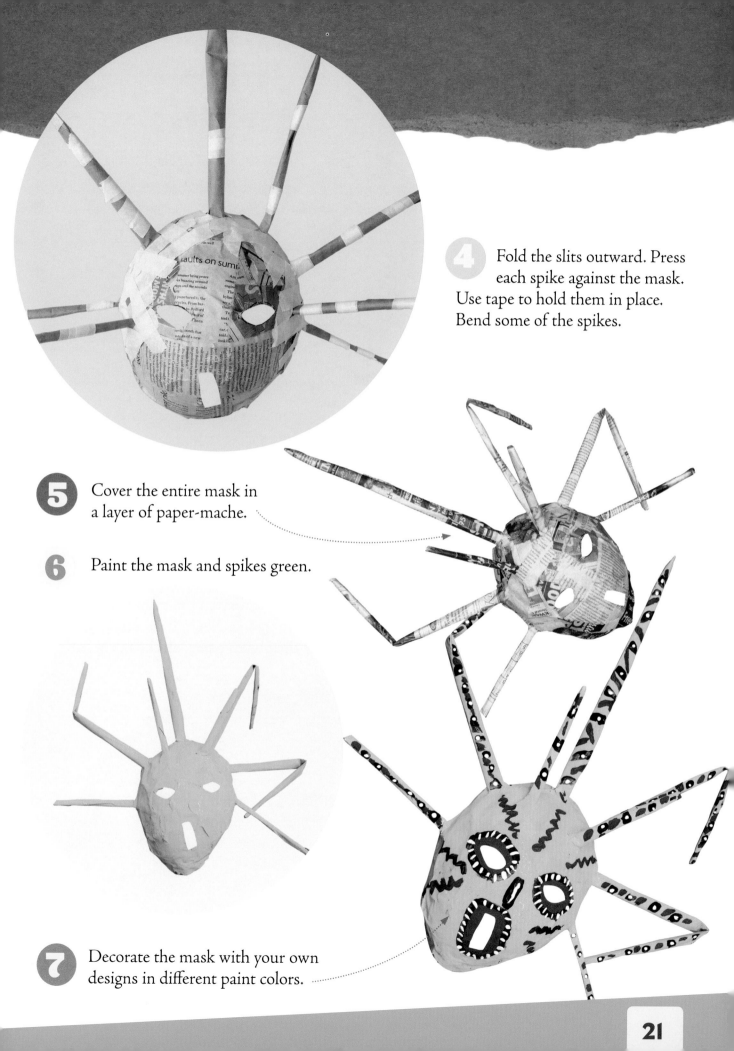

4 Fold the slits outward. Press each spike against the mask. Use tape to hold them in place. Bend some of the spikes.

5 Cover the entire mask in a layer of paper-mache.

6 Paint the mask and spikes green.

7 Decorate the mask with your own designs in different paint colors.

BUNNY MASK

You'll Need:

✔ Half-balloon mask base
✔ Scissors
✔ Paper towel strips
✔ Paper-mache glue
✔ Cardboard
✔ Paint and paintbrush
✔ Pink pipe cleaners

1 Make a half-balloon mask base using strips of paper towel (see pages 6–7). Cut out two eyes.

2 Use the patterns on page 30 to cut out two ears and teeth from cardboard. Cover them with paper-mache as shown.

3 Tape the ears to the top of the mask. For the nose, make a small ball out of paper-mache. Use your hands to press it together. Make two larger balls for cheeks. Glue cardboard teeth to the bottom of the mask. Cover the entire face with paper-mache. Let it dry.

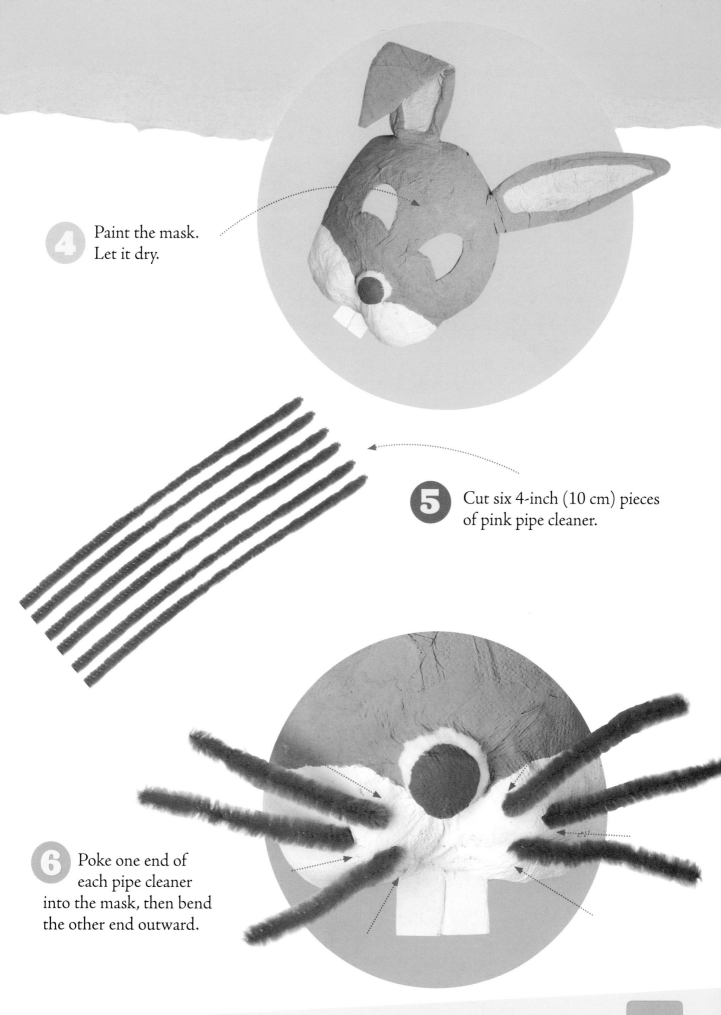

4 Paint the mask.
Let it dry.

5 Cut six 4-inch (10 cm) pieces
of pink pipe cleaner.

6 Poke one end of
each pipe cleaner
into the mask, then bend
the other end outward.

BIRD MASK

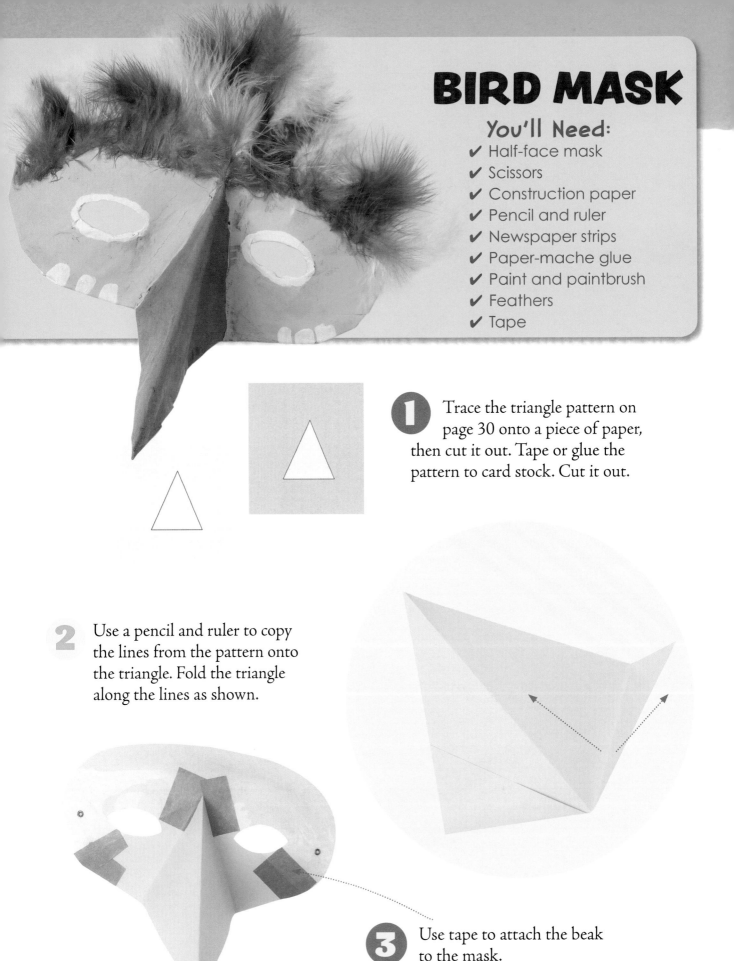

You'll Need:
✔ Half-face mask
✔ Scissors
✔ Construction paper
✔ Pencil and ruler
✔ Newspaper strips
✔ Paper-mache glue
✔ Paint and paintbrush
✔ Feathers
✔ Tape

1 Trace the triangle pattern on page 30 onto a piece of paper, then cut it out. Tape or glue the pattern to card stock. Cut it out.

2 Use a pencil and ruler to copy the lines from the pattern onto the triangle. Fold the triangle along the lines as shown.

3 Use tape to attach the beak to the mask.

4 Cover the mask with paper-mache. Make sure to cover the bottom of the beak, too. Let it dry.

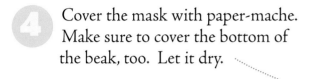

5 Paint the mask. Leave to dry.

Glue feathers to the top

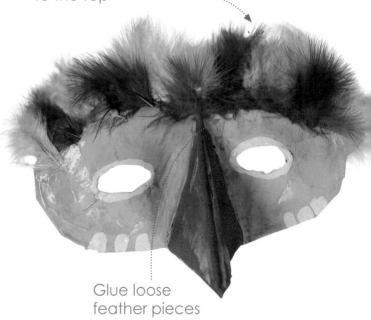

6 Spread glue along the top edge of the mask. Glue colorful feathers to the top. Use scissors to cut one or two orange feathers into little pieces. Add more glue along the edge of the row of feathers. Glue the loose pieces to cover the edge of the first row of feathers.

Glue loose feather pieces

7 Cut a piece of tape, then stick four feathers to it. Tape the feathers onto the back of the mask in the center of the top edge.

ALIEN MASK

You'll Need:

- ✔ Half-balloon mask base
- ✔ Scissors
- ✔ Paper towel strips
- ✔ Paper-mache glue
- ✔ Paint and paintbrush
- ✔ Metallic pipe cleaners
- ✔ Tape
- ✔ Fake jewels
- ✔ Googly eye (optional)

1 Make a half-balloon mask base using strips of paper towel (see pages 6–7). Draw and cut out eyes, nostrils, and a mouth.

2 Adding an extra eye is optional. To make the eye, form a wad using paper towel and glue. Squeeze out any extra glue. Shape the wad into an eye shape as shown. Use the same steps to make a small eyeball. Place it on top of the eye. Let it dry.

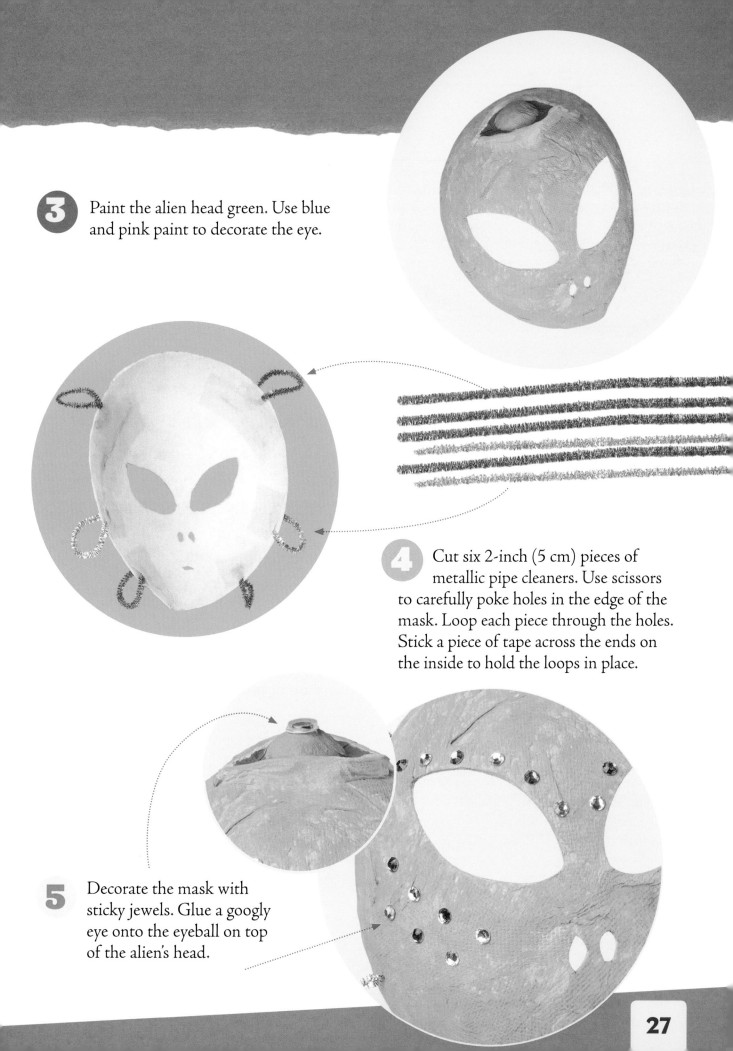

3 Paint the alien head green. Use blue and pink paint to decorate the eye.

4 Cut six 2-inch (5 cm) pieces of metallic pipe cleaners. Use scissors to carefully poke holes in the edge of the mask. Loop each piece through the holes. Stick a piece of tape across the ends on the inside to hold the loops in place.

5 Decorate the mask with sticky jewels. Glue a googly eye onto the eyeball on top of the alien's head.

UPSIDE-DOWN FACE MASK

You'll Need:

- ✔ Full-face mask base
- ✔ Scissors
- ✔ Newspaper strips
- ✔ Paper towels
- ✔ Paper-mache glue
- ✔ Paint and paintbrush

1 Start with a full-face plastic mask.

2 Cover the mask with paper-mache. Fill the eyes and form face features such as lips and eyebrows with wads of paper-mache. Let it dry.

3 Poke two holes to see through just above the mouth.

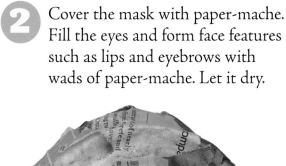

4 Use strips of paper towel to make hair. Shape it with your hand, pressing firmly against the mask. Let it dry.

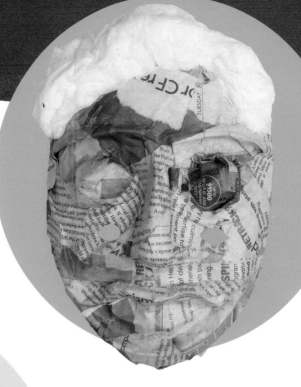

5 Paint the mask. Start with a base layer of any skin color. When the paint dries, add eyes, eyebrows, hair, and lips. Don't forget to paint some nice white teeth!

6 When you put on the mask, make sure the face is upside down!

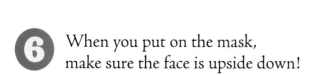

PATTERNS

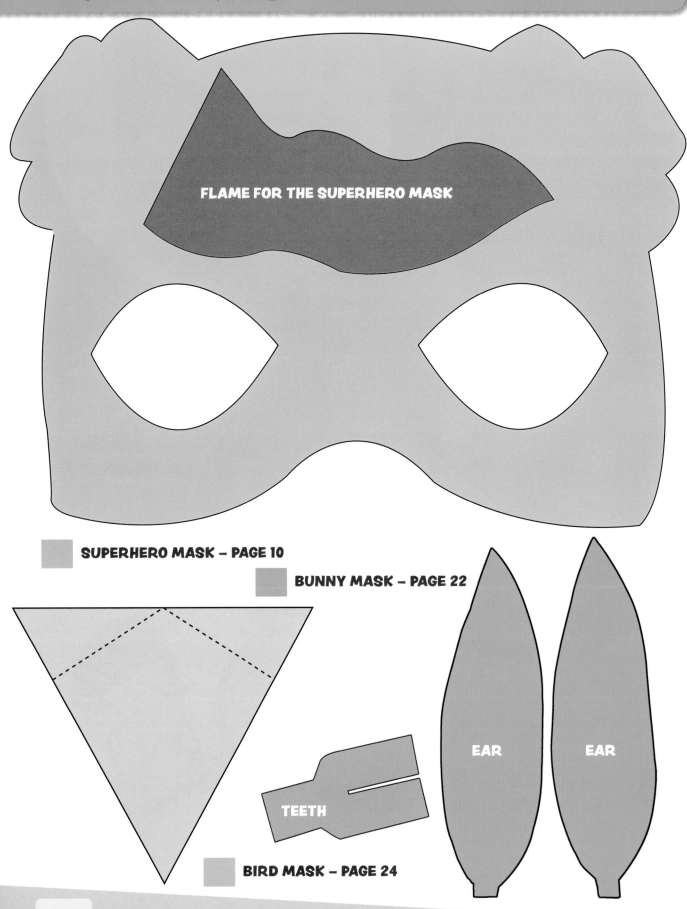

FLAME FOR THE SUPERHERO MASK

SUPERHERO MASK – PAGE 10

BUNNY MASK – PAGE 22

TEETH

EAR

EAR

BIRD MASK – PAGE 24

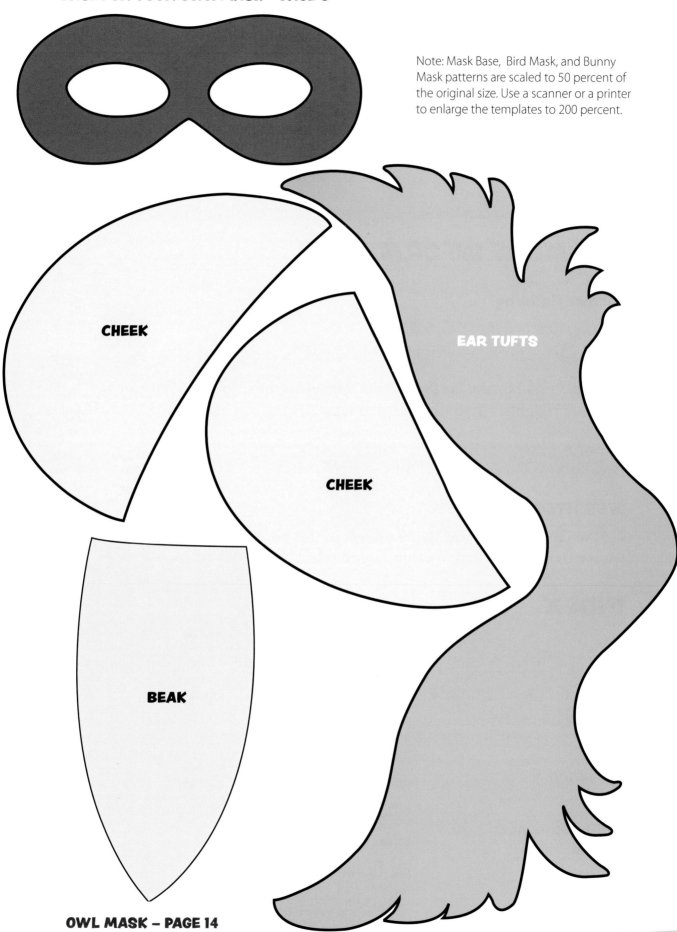

BASE FOR YOUR OWN MASK – PAGE 8

Note: Mask Base, Bird Mask, and Bunny Mask patterns are scaled to 50 percent of the original size. Use a scanner or a printer to enlarge the templates to 200 percent.

CHEEK

EAR TUFTS

CHEEK

BEAK

OWL MASK – PAGE 14

GLOSSARY

base Something that supports something else.

helmet A protective head covering made of hard material that protects one's head.

mold An object that a material is placed on or in to make a specific shape.

piñatas Decorated containers that are filled with candy, then cracked open with sticks.

FOR MORE INFORMATION

Further Reading

Kenney, Karen. *Super Simple Masks.*
Edina, MN: ABDO Publishing Company, 2009.

Plomer, Anna Llimos. *Earth-Friendly Papier-Mâché Crafts in 5 Easy Steps.*
Berkeley Heights, NJ : Enslow Elementary, 2013.

Schwake, Susan. *3D Art Lab for Kids.*
Beverly, MA: Quarry Books, 2013.

WEBSITES

For web resources related to the subject of this book, go to: www.windmillbooks.com/weblinks and select this book's title.

INDEX